Along the Way

Selected writings
by
John M. Ketterer

Avid Readers Publishing Group

Lakewood, California

Along the Way

Avid Readers Publishing Group

http://www.avidreaderspg.com

ISBN-13: 978-1-935105-12-1

Printed in the United States

Contents

Along the Way

I love
the quiet
sheltered harbor
and
the yawning
sunny beaches
but today
i want
to sail out
into deep waters
where everything
unknown
is waiting
and where
the possibility
of becoming
more
than i am
is
everywhere.

Life

sweeps before us

in grand

infinite gestures

only

the heart

can truly

keep pace.

Love

is the Rosetta Stone

between

you and life.

Strange
new butterfly
with iridescent
wings and spirit

when
i watch
your flight
vibrant worlds
appear

magical
metamorphosis
has altered
the outer form
yet your timeless
inner essence
remains the same

you

are of the

earth

of the stars

and all

the moments

in between

i feel

your pulsing

sensitivity

your secret dreams

are invisible

tattoos

on my soul

which

i hand color

in the

deep forest far.

You
are the anchor
of my focus

the calm
in the eye
of my journey

you are
the truth
in my heart

i am
reminded of this
each time
i light
a candle
and
watch
the darkness
disappear.

When
the colors
of life
around you
are bright
and intense
you
are painting
with your
inner palette.

Sometimes
the wind
changes direction
yet it still
remains the wind

sometimes
the bird
stops flapping
and glides
yet it is still flying

sometimes
i'm out of step
yet i'm still
walking

sometimes
i'm like
a chameleon
yet deep down
i'm still me.

The only
crisis you have
is a crisis
of the heart

as you
move away
from the heart
you move away
from the center
of your
true power.

The idea
is not
to lose yourself
in love

rather
to find
yourself
through
love.

Even
small acts
of kindness
and compassion
although unattended
by disclosure or
rewards
still do not go
unnoticed
as they are
poured into
the vast
pool of love
through the
vessels
of our heart
and
come together
in our
collective
consciousness
and do
make a difference

little streams
pour into

larger streams
then into rivers
and into
mighty oceans
of wondrous
powerful love.

W e
   can feel
      many losses
         in our life

the
    biggest loss
       is not following
         your true path
           and what is
             in your heart.

We have all
worn the shoes of fear

now we must
step into
the slippers of grace.

When
    we are
        in tune
            with ourselves

we have
    a career
        in the music
          of life.

When
you are free

you live without
a safety net.

Flow me out
to sea
in the hush
of night
then
let the wind
lift me
to the heavenly
stars

let the
immenseness of life
fill my senses
and
let this moment
be one of
many more
to come.

P erhaps
all the King's horses
and
all the King's men
couldn't put
Humpty
back together again
but
deep down inside
Humpty knew
he could.

I am crane

i glide
    in deep blue
    and pillow white

i feel
    velvet wind
    father sun
    universal heartbeat

seek me out
in the sky
as
i reflect
your desire
for freedom
back to you

and
for a moment
you can
be me
and i you.

I am panther

i am
  true stealth
i am
  true fire

i am wild
  with freedom
i am wild
  with aliveness

my movement
  is bold
  committed
  to the ancient
  spark of life

i know my path
i know who
i am.

The Long Embrace

A

distant prayer

closer

and

closer

it comes

until

at last...

you.

Your timeless
   unfiltered innocence
   brushes aside
   all temporal realms
   and penetrates
   into the
   inner altars
   of my soul

your gaze
   dissolves all
   that is untrue

perhaps
   i cannot
   keep you forever
   but i'm
   going to try.

I loved you
before I knew you

my heart
sent out
a message

you answered
the call.

Your essence
falls like
a drop of water
into my consciousness
and ripples outward
in perfect harmony
to all aspects
of myself.

With you
i experienced
a thousand
lifetimes
in just
one
moment.

Your spirit
sweeps through
my life
and gathers
all the restless tears
and valleys of uneasiness

i am reborn
in gratitude.

You are the
moon lily
floating in
my mind

whether day
or darkest night
your presence
is felt
and gives
soothing comfort
on my journey.

Your soft eyes
    fill up the sky
until i am showered
    with your
        heavenly glow

your movement
    in my life
leaves a trail
    of golden
        precious moments

your sweet love
launches a
thousand lighted
paper lanterns
into the mists
of endless time

your heartbeat signals
your presence
in the vast
tapestry of souls
so i can find you
on this quiet
and jeweled night.

Why don't you
whisper in my ear

let me feel
your eternal flame
that burns in my heart

let our souls embrace.

Let me sit by
your bedside
and hold your
delicate hand

let's wander
between the
sheets of time
to some enchanted shore

let wave after wave
of infinity
wash over us.

Come
let's collect the berries
and small wildflowers
in the forests and
along the roadside

let's be aimless
let us just flow
in the gentle
sweet currents
of the heart.

River walk
down to the sea

the sound of my footsteps on the
earth sets my mind free

thoughts of you
set my heart free.

We
take in
the breath of spring

we feel
the message
in our hearts

the moments unfold
and we are drawn down
the path of spring
again and again.

Enter The Goddess
with a flaming
heart of passion

silencing all your thoughts
except those focused
on her sweet charm
and depth of mystery

you must enter
her unfolding story

peer into her eyes
and she will
tell all.

Caress me
    with your
        essence
let it
    carry me

to your
    enchanted
        world.

The light
over the heather
honors me so
and
the gentle breeze
strongly moves
my heart until
the memory of you
is in full view.

Take
the most fragrant tea
the brightest gem
the dew from a blade of grass
the golden notes
of an inspired heart
the dancing light upon the sea

send these precious things
to my love
and let them speak loudly
for me.

Please
linger long
in my heart
with your sweetness

be there
when I return home
and open
the door.

Listen
while I explain
to you
what is in my heart

please be patient

it may take
several lifetimes.

Heart

Ancient travelers
used the stars
at night
to guide them
on their journey

someday
all we will need
to find our way
will be the light
in our hearts.

Love
blooms
in the heart

timeless

like
the wind
as it
comes and goes
yet never leaves
for it brings
the breath of life

so it is
with love
    the fastener
    of all things

the healer
of all things
broken

the inspiration
of all things
imagined

the reason
for all things
to exist.

We are all patrons
of the moment

voyeurs
of the unexpected
in an ocean
of strange vibrant
energy
which we slowly tame
with our heart.

The heart
translates the unknown
into the known.

The morning light
lets us see

true hearts
see further.

We are shifting
from a thirst
of material things
to a thirst
for things spiritual

from the seen
to the unseen

from the mind
to the heart.

My mind
wanders
to your door

my heart
opens it.

We return
to familiar themes

themes of the heart

these are the truest
pleasures for our
native soul

themes that bring
light to our path
in life

themes that make
sense of it all.

We are

in the process

of

resetting

to our hearts

resetting

from minds

of fear

and scarcity

resetting

from

towering emotional

shadows

which short-circuit

our

souls.

We
are all looking
for our place
in the sun
yet deeper down
we need to find
our place in our hearts
where the doors
of abundance
open wide
and fills your life
with earthly
and heavenly treasures.

Home
is
the
person
who
lives
in
their
heart

for
it
is
there
we
all
must
truly
reside.

Life
knocks at your door

fear keeps the
door closed

the heart opens
the door wide.

People
get inundated
swept away
by the contents
of their minds

how will it feel
when we are
swept away by
the ecstatic streams
of the heart?

We usually
put our trust
in the architecture
of the mind

our trust
should be placed
in the heart
no matter how vulnerable
this makes us feel.

Sometimes
life becomes
cloudy

we are forced
it seems
to see in the dark

our only
true course
is to trust
the light
in our hearts.

Words
    not connected
        to the heart
are like lost
children
searching for
their home.

The
Divine
Heart

connects
the many
to the
One.

I did not have
a camera to capture
the brilliant full moon

yet its presence
still rises
in my heart.

If
you have questions
look deep
into the heart
for it cannot lie

if
you can find
your heart
you can
find the truth.

The
trade winds
took you
from my eyes
but not
my heart.

Haiku Journey

Falling
    golden
        leaves

so many
    messages

all at once.

A leaf
floats and twirls
in the wind

final destination
is unknown

the journey
is everything.

Outside
a presence

the trees sway
and rustle

enchanted wind.

The breeze
lifts my spirit

i send it
on tiptoe
to your window

ambassador
from my
heart.

Work ends
sun fades

best time
of the day
arrives

sound of your
footsteps.

You move
among my thoughts

like the scent
of rose petals

your eyes
shining.

City noise fades

the night casts
a long shadow

cricket orchestra.

Sometimes
you appear

like the moon

reflecting
on deep
mysterious
waters.

I hear your song
      i feel your heart

you weave a story
      that i must read

a story i must live.

Y ou are
    imprinted
        on my life

as
i
unfold

so does
    your
        presence.

I
spread out
bedding

prepare
for dream time

nights journey
draws near.

If life

is a dream

let me be

a master dreamer

and let me

dream of you

forever.

Morning
comes to visit

eyes open
from night's sleep

who am i
today?

Sunrise and quiet

dream world
clings to the spirit

sweet night's reverie.

Yesterday

fades away

at night
i dream
i laugh

in morning
harmony restored.

I prepare green tea

brown earthen cup
is waiting

calm is at the door.

Heavy
snow
covers
village

uncovers
silence.

Falling snow

    mind vanishes

i remain.

Deep
piles of snow

deep piles
of quiet

deeply
i breathe
the joy
the beauty.

Winter

quiet

heartbeat.

Beautiful
snowflakes
layer deep
outside

i cannot invite
them in

they will vanish
by the fire.

Every snowflake
　is unique

each falls
　separately

together
　a powerful
　winter.

Blizzard outside

travel impossible

i go within

go everywhere.

Winter
is total

winter is harsh

we all become
brothers and sisters.

Thick
low hanging
fog

mountain tops
look like
islands

we are
transported.

Winding
mountain path

unused in
recent times

still full of
ancient travelers.

Dark clouds
thunder

sound
of rain
approaches

intermission
from a chattering
mind.

Storm clouds

people seek shelter

plants rejoice.

F lash storm
in city

strong pelting rains
in downtown

umbrella forest.

Raindrops
fall from sky

tall reed sways
in forest pond

dragonfly condo.

Cat
   sleeps

what is
      she
            dreaming?

i join her
      to find out.

Finally

spring leaps
from my mind

and
greets my eyes.

Bird
on
branch

song
in
the
wind

simplicity.

Beautiful
flowered meadow

forested
green hills
rise up

an invitation
to the heart.

T all
and silent

reincarnated
warriors

bamboo forest.

Full moon
and strong
winds

rice fields
become
ocean waves

the heart goes surfing.

F ield
of wildflowers

look closely
with your
heart

see the
reflection
of your own
beauty.

How the summer
dances in my heart

hold my hand

and it will dance
in yours.

Sky unfolds

mind guiets

i unfold.

Dawn

polished stones
along the
misty shore

we gather
the treasures.

The waves wash
over the rocks
again and again

all my senses
come alive

i arrive
again and again.

Golden sands
blue skies

thoughts drift out
over the sea

like kites
dancing
in the wind.

When
mind mailbox
becomes too full

follow
the path
to the sea

then peace
will follow
you home.

Philosopher's Café

There is a lot
   of magic
      in the world

the truest magic
   is being your
      true self

and allowing
   the miracle of life
      to flow through you.

We know

yet sometimes
we suffer

because
we don't
follow through
with what
we know.

Sometimes
it seems
the world
will cut you
to shreds
if you
come out
and express
your true self
your true feelings

but the only
fragile illusion
is your personality

your spirit
    is forever shining
        forever bright
with unlimited
possibilities.

Everyone
    wants to be loved
everyone
    wants to be heard

things get twisted

we need to work on this.

Your
   lasting freedom
      joy
         happiness

   is not gathered
      by finding someone
         who will provide
         those things

   but rather finding
      them in
         yourself.

Some
of us
become bent
twisted
by life's process

it takes
great resolve
to hold onto
this illusion

if you
let go
you will
spring back
into your
original
pure
self.

All manner
of things
are present
and come forward
into view
    into the senses

what you call
    good and bad
    all are present

it is preference
    and choice
    that makes
them stay
    or vanish
        in the
            sunlight.

After
a long trip
it feels good
to be home
and sleep
in your own bed

returning to
your true self
has the same
feeling of
being home.

If
something is
missing
you do not have
far to travel

the
lost and found
department
is within
you.

The information
you are seeking
is always available

truth is
always available.

The peace
    you are seeking
    is found
    inside yourself

the beautiful
    places you want
    to visit
    starts with
    creating a
    beautiful place
    inside yourself

the wonderful
    relationship
    you desire
    first starts by
    having a relationship
    with yourself

make peace
with who you
really are

love who
you are

be true
to who you are.

We are at the gates
of the core engine
of creation

we pass through
by opening our hearts
full wide no limits
unbound by fear
which now is smiling
because it too
has brought gifts
which in many
cases were unopened
unexamined
and unclaimed.

War
impacts the lives
of many
in painful
chaotic ways

also
a setting
brilliant sun
can impact
the lives of many

war
tears the heart
of mankind

a setting sun
restores it.

In truth
we are always
whole

we become diluted
from our original essence
by various acquired
beliefs, fears
and forgetfulness

in truth
we are not
really shaped
by the outer world
but by the inner world.

In everyone's heart
there is a jewel

we search
for this jewel

at last
the jewel is found

we marvel
at its beauty
brilliance
majesty

closer and closer
we admire
its wondrous
existence

until
at last
we become
the jewel
again.

What
do we have
but
who we
really are?

our
essence
is precious

our
essence
is everything

a
treasure
beyond compare

the
soul's
infinite journey
to
self awareness
self love.

Today
is within today
and tomorrow lies
waiting in the jungle

yesterday follows behind
hungry for your mind.

The last time I saw you
is still swimming in my mind

sometimes it does the backstroke
and drives me insane.

Swift is thought
taken far out into the
night and spent
among the stars
and recaptured
at sunrise
by me.

The waterfront
of the soul

entering into
the very depths
of beingness

passing through
the walls of fear

riding the heart waves
to core essence

a vastness so deep
it humbles all.

Listen

laughter calls
to us

it beckons us
to follow

trace its smile
upon your heart

let it bring you
into the mirrors
of your soul
where you
can look at you

the perfect expression
of all that is
and yet to come.

We are more
than tiny specks
on a tiny isle
in the universe

we are the specs
we are the universe

when you know this
you are free
you are infinite
you are endless.

You are the door
to yourself

you are what's
in front of the door

you are what's
behind the door.

It's not
WHERE you are

but rather
where *YOU* are.

Your thoughts

your passions

your dreams

are sacred

you are sacred

believe it

speak it

be it.

We are all
translating
God

sometimes
God seems to be
lost in the translation.

We
are all masters
of our destiny
whether
we are
aware of it
or not.

We
are all
in the process
of reconnecting
to our true source
our true heritage
our true home
our infinite self.

To manifest
anything
you must first
manifest
your true self
your true heart.

Fear puts limits
on all that is

expectations
put boundaries
on all that could be.

Fear destroys
the fabric
of life

love

weaves it

back together.

Peace
is
simple

life
is
complex.

Our
imagination
is our
angel.

Life
is intricate

subtle

take heed

of the winds

of change

if overlooked

hurricanes

of magnitude

can manifest.

Keep your
vision pure

keep your
vision clear

keep your
vision of
the true you.

It's not

about surviving

it's about creating

it's about passion

it's about imagination.

We store

a lot of information

in our mind

we forget

who programmed it.

How can

an illusion

be more powerful

than its creator?

only in the mind.

Every moment
can be extraordinary
if you are present.

As we become

more and more aware

of the importance of

being our true self

the expression "truth or

consequences"

takes on greater and greater

meaning.

See not

good or bad

see only choice.

What irritates you
about another person
has nothing to do
with them
but everything
to do with you.

Those

who are guided

by greed

are really guided

by fear.

Just as

releasing toxic

chemicals into

the air

so does thinking

negative thoughts

release toxins

into the world.

The deepest communication
is the art of saying nothing
but meaning
everything.

Face your fears

as your friends

as guides

to the parts of you

that need

to be brought into

the LIGHT.

Beyond
the limits
is where life
really begins.

Fear

only invades

those who

fear.

Life is rich

become rich
by knowing this.

Be love

then it

will always

be with you.

Printed in the United States
126278LV00002B/250-282/P

9 781935 105121